Let's Learn To Prompt

Dr. Kevin Abankwa

ISBN: 979-8-9879189-0-6

DEDICATION

To my amazing wife, Awo and wonderful children, Kenji, Kayden, and Kaila. Your unwavering support for me in my pursuit for knowledge and sharing knowledge is what keeps me going every day.

CONTENTS

1 Introduction to Generative AI And Prompting 7

2 Core Principles of Effective Prompting 12

3 Types of Prompts 17

4 Techniques to Improve Prompting 22

5 Practical Applications of Prompting 28

6 Common Challenges in Prompting 33

7 Ethical Use of Generative AI 38

8 Prompt Engineering: A Look Ahead 44

9 Multiple-Choice Questions And Answers 50

1. INTRODUCTION TO GENERATIVE AI AND PROMPTING

What is Generative AI?

Generative Artificial Intelligence (AI) refers to a category of AI models that can generate new content, such as text, images, music, or even videos, based on the input they receive. Unlike traditional AI systems that perform tasks like classification or predictions, generative AI is designed to create outputs that are creative and original.

Some common examples of generative AI tools include:

- Text Generation: Tools like ChatGPT and Google Bard can produce essays, stories, summaries, and more.
- Image Generation: Tools like DALL·E and MidJourney create images from textual descriptions.
- Music and Audio: AI tools like Jukebox generate new pieces of music.

Generative AI models are trained on vast datasets, learning patterns and relationships within the data.

When you provide a prompt (a request or input), the AI generates an output based on its training.

Example:

- Prompt: "Write a short story about a dog who loves flowers."
- AI Output: "Once upon a time, in a peaceful valley, there lived a dog named Fern who adored flowers more than gold..."

What is Prompting in Generative AI?

Prompting is the process of providing clear and effective input (called a prompt) to generative AI systems to achieve the desired output. A well-crafted prompt ensures the AI understands what you want and generates relevant and accurate content.

Why is Prompting Important?

1. Quality of Output: A clear and specific prompt produces better results.
2. Efficiency: Well-structured prompts save time by reducing trial and error.
3. Creative Control: Users can guide AI to produce content in a specific style, tone, or format.

Why Do Prompts Matter for Beginners?

For beginners, learning how to prompt effectively is crucial to:

- Get the most out of generative AI tools.
- Avoid frustration caused by vague or irrelevant AI responses.
- Explore new and creative possibilities with AI.

Think of prompting like giving instructions to a talented chef. The clearer your instructions (e.g., "Make me a vegan pasta with spinach and mushrooms"), the better the dish will match your expectations.

Practical Exercise: Your First Prompt

Let's try a simple exercise to introduce you to prompting. If you have access to a generative AI tool like ChatGPT, follow these steps:

1. Open your AI tool.
2. Enter the following prompt: "Explain what generative AI is in simple terms suitable for a beginner."
3. Observe the AI's response and note how clear and beginner-friendly it is.

Multiple-Choice Questions: Introduction to Generative AI and Prompting

1. What is Generative AI primarily designed to do?
   A) Predict weather patterns
   B) Generate creative content such as text and images
   C) Sort and classify data
   D) Perform calculations

2. Which of the following tools is used for image generation?
   A) ChatGPT
   B) Google Bard
   C) MidJourney
   D) Jukebox

3. What is a prompt in the context of generative AI?
   A) The result generated by the AI
   B) A clear input provided to guide the AI's output
   C) A tool used to train AI systems
   D) A dataset used for AI modeling

4. Why is prompting compared to giving instructions to a chef?

   A) Because it involves cooking skills

   B) To highlight that vague prompts yield poor results

   C) To emphasize the importance of AI tools in restaurants

   D) Because prompts need to be followed precisely like recipes

5. What is the main benefit of learning how to prompt effectively?

   A) It helps AI predict the future

   B) It reduces the need for creativity

   C) It produces better and more relevant AI outputs

   D) It trains AI models faster

Answers

1. B 2. C 3. B 4. B 5. C

2. CORE PRINCIPLES OF EFFECTIVE PROMPTING

Clarity and Specificity

The foundation of an effective prompt lies in being clear and specific. Ambiguous or vague prompts often lead to irrelevant or incomplete outputs.

Key Aspects of Clarity:

1. State the Objective: Clearly communicate what you want the AI to produce.

o Example:

- **Vague Prompt:** "Write about dogs."
- **Clear Prompt:** "Write a 200-word paragraph about the history of Golden Retrievers as family pets."

2. Include Details: Add specific instructions such as format, tone, or style.

o Example:

Prompt: "Write a short, humorous poem about a cat chasing a butterfly."

3. Avoid Overloading Information: Break complex prompts into smaller parts when necessary.

Provide Context

Generative AI systems perform better when given sufficient background or context.

Examples of Providing Context:

- **Without Context:** "Summarize this document."
- **With Context:** "Summarize this research article in 3 bullet points for a college student studying biology."

The additional context (audience and format) allows the AI to generate a more relevant and tailored response.

Iterative Refinement

Improving a prompt often involves testing and refining it iteratively. If the first response is not satisfactory, tweak the prompt for better results.

<u>Steps for Refining Prompts:</u>

1. Identify what is missing or incorrect in the output.
2. Add more details or clarify ambiguous instructions.
3. Experiment with alternative phrasing.

Practical Exercise: Craft a Clear Prompt

Try the following exercise:

1. Open your generative AI tool.
2. Input the following vague prompt: "Tell me about space."

3. Observe the output.
4. Now refine the prompt to: "Write a 100-word summary of the solar system for a middle school science class."
5. Compare the two outputs and note the improvements.

Multiple-Choice Questions: Core Principles of Effective Prompting

1. What is the most important aspect of a clear prompt?

   A) Ambiguity

   B) Specificity and clarity

   C) Length

   D) Creativity

2. What does providing context in a prompt do?

   A) Confuses the AI

   B) Reduces the quality of output

   C) Helps the AI tailor the response appropriately

   D) Makes the prompt shorter

3. What is an example of iterative refinement in prompting?

   A) Giving up after the first result

   B) Testing, tweaking, and improving the prompt over time

   C) Using only short prompts

   D) Ignoring AI output entirely

4. Why should you avoid overloading a prompt with information?

   A) It makes the AI faster

   B) Complex prompts can confuse the AI

   C) AI prefers shorter prompts

   D) AI cannot handle multiple sentences

5. Which of the following prompts provides the best clarity?

   A) "Write about history."

   B) "Write a 150-word summary about World War II events for high school students."

   C) "Tell me something."

   D) "Talk about wars."

Answers

1.B 2.C 3. B 4. B 5. B

3. TYPES OF PROMPTS

Generative AI tools respond to user inputs, or prompts, to generate outputs. Understanding the various types of prompts is essential for achieving accurate and effective results. Prompts can be broadly categorized into the following types:

1. **Instruction-Based Prompts**

Instruction-based prompts explicitly direct the AI to perform a task. These prompts are clear and specific, often starting with action verbs like "write," "create," "summarize," or "generate."

- Example: "Summarize the following paragraph in 3 bullet points."
- When to Use: When you need structured or task-specific output, such as summaries, reports, or instructions.

2. **Question-Based Prompts**

Question-based prompts are framed as questions to elicit specific information or responses. These prompts are excellent for gathering facts, opinions, or detailed explanations.

- Example: "What are the causes of climate change?"
- When to Use: When you need factual or explanatory outputs.

3. **Contextual Prompts**

Contextual prompts provide background information to guide the AI's response. They are useful when you want the AI to understand specific circumstances, tone, or roles.

- Example: "You are a history teacher explaining World War II to a group of 12-year-olds. Describe the main events in simple terms."
- When to Use: When a tailored response is required, such as role-playing or creative storytelling.

4. **Open-Ended Prompts**

Open-ended prompts allow the AI to explore a topic without strict constraints. These prompts encourage creativity, brainstorming, or idea generation.

- Example: "Write a story about a time traveler who lands in ancient Egypt."
- When to Use: When creativity or ideation is the goal.

5. **Data-Based Prompts**

Data-based prompts involve presenting structured data or specific inputs to generate AI-driven analysis or insights.

- Example: "Based on the data below, provide a brief analysis of sales trends for Q1."
- When to Use: When you are working with data-heavy

tasks, such as trends analysis, charts, or calculations.

6. **Chain-of-Thought Prompts**

Chain-of-thought prompts break a complex task into smaller steps, prompting the AI to solve the task step by step. This improves reasoning and accuracy.

- Example: "To calculate the cost of a project, first list all expenses. Then add them to determine the total cost."
- When to Use: For multi-step tasks requiring logical reasoning, such as problem-solving or math.

7. **Few-Shot Prompts**

Few-shot prompts provide a few examples of inputs and desired outputs to help the AI understand the pattern or expected format.

- Example:
  - Input: "Translate 'Hello' to French."
  - Output: "Bonjour"
  - Input: "Translate 'Thank you' to French."
  - Output: "Merci"
  - Input: "Translate 'Goodbye' to French."

- When to Use: When the desired output format is unfamiliar or needs clarification.

Multiple-Choice Questions: Types of Prompts

1. Which of the following is an example of an instruction-based prompt?

A) "Write a summary of the article in 5 sentences."

B) "What is the importance of photosynthesis?"

C) "Describe the history of Rome in the style of a poem."

D) "Generate a story about a dragon living in a forest."

2. When should you use a contextual prompt?

A) To generate structured, step-by-step tasks.

B) To provide tailored responses with specific roles or scenarios.

C) To gather factual and explanatory information.

D) To present AI with structured data for analysis.

3. What distinguishes open-ended prompts from other types of prompts?

A) They require specific tasks to be completed.

B) They focus on providing data analysis.

C) They encourage creative and exploratory responses.

D) They involve providing role-based scenarios.

4. Which type of prompt involves breaking tasks into logical steps?

A) Few-shot prompts

B) Chain-of-thought prompts

C) Question-based prompts

D) Instruction-based prompts

5. Few-shot prompts are useful when:

A) You want the AI to generate creative content.

B) You provide examples of input-output patterns for clarity.

C) You need AI to handle data-based tasks.

D) You require exploratory or brainstorming responses.

Answers

1. A 2.B 3. C 4. B 5. B

4. TECHNIQUES TO IMPROVE PROMPTING

Improving the quality of your prompts ensures better and more consistent AI-generated results. Here are proven techniques to help you master effective prompting:

1. <u>Be Clear and Specific</u>

The clearer your instructions, the better the response. Avoid vague prompts and instead provide specific tasks, goals, or guidelines.

- Example of a Vague Prompt: "Tell me about dogs."
- Improved Prompt: "Provide a brief summary of the most common dog breeds and their characteristics."

2. <u>Add Context</u>

Including relevant context helps the AI produce tailored responses. Context can involve the intended audience, role, tone, or purpose.

- Example: "Write a 150-word email to a client explaining a delayed project, keeping the tone apologetic yet professional."

3. <u>Use Step-by-Step Instructions (Chain-of-Thought)</u>

Breaking tasks into sequential steps helps the AI handle

complex queries more effectively.

- Example: "Step 1: Identify the main causes of inflation. Step 2: Explain each cause in 2-3 sentences."

4. Specify Output Format

Defining the structure or format of the output reduces ambiguity.

- Example: "List the benefits of exercise in bullet points, with no more than 8 points."

5. Iterate and Refine

If the first output isn't satisfactory, refine your prompt by adding more details, rephrasing, or clarifying the goal.

- Example: If the prompt "Explain machine learning" produces overly technical content, refine it to: "Explain machine learning to a high school student using simple terms and examples."

6. Use Examples for Few-Shot Learning

Provide input-output examples to clarify the expected results. This is especially helpful when working with AI on unique or unfamiliar tasks.

- Example:
  - Input: "Turn the following sentence into a metaphor: 'She works very hard.'"
  - Output: "She's a blazing comet, burning through tasks with unstoppable force."

7. Set Boundaries or Constraints

Constraints help focus the AI's output on specific requirements, such as word limits, tone, or themes.

- Example: "Describe artificial intelligence in exactly 50 words."

8. Use Role-Playing for Contextual Prompts

Asking the AI to assume a role can add perspective and focus to its response.

- Example: "You are a customer service agent responding to an angry customer about a delayed product shipment. Write a professional and empathetic response."

9. Leverage Follow-Up Prompts

When the AI's initial response needs improvement, follow up with clarifications or further instructions.

- Example: "That's great, but can you expand on point 3 with more examples?"

10. Experiment with Variations

Rephrase or experiment with your prompts to explore different angles or ideas. Slight changes in wording can yield varied responses.

- Example:
  - Prompt 1: "List 5 tips for improving time management."
  - Prompt 2: "How can someone improve their time management skills?"

Multiple-Choice Questions: Techniques to Improve Prompting

1. Why is it important to provide clear and specific prompts?

A) It allows the AI to be more creative.

B) It ensures that the AI understands and meets the task requirements.

C) It reduces the need for follow-up prompts.

D) It makes the output longer and more detailed.

2. What is the benefit of adding context to a prompt?

A) It simplifies complex tasks into smaller steps.

B) It helps tailor the AI's response to a specific tone, role, or audience.

C) It allows the AI to brainstorm ideas freely.

D) It speeds up the AI's response time.

3. What is the main purpose of breaking down complex prompts into smaller parts?

A) To confuse the AI system

B) To make the output more manageable and accurate

C) To make the prompt more creative

D) To generate random responses

4. Which of the following techniques can help improve the specificity of a prompt?

A) Using vague and general instructions

B) Adding clear details such as format, tone, and context

C) Repeating the same prompt multiple times

D) Using only one-word prompts

5. What should you do if the AI's output does not meet your expectations?

A) Stop using the AI tool

B) Rephrase and refine the prompt with more clarity and detail

C) Provide less context in the next prompt

D) Use multiple AI tools at the same time

Answers

1. B   2. B   3. B   4. B   5. B

5. PRACTICAL APPLICATIONS OF PROMPTING

Prompting is a powerful tool in the realm of generative AI, enabling users to harness the potential of AI systems to complete tasks ranging from simple content creation to complex problem-solving. In this section, I will share with you a few key practical applications where effective prompting can make a significant impact.

Content Creation

Generative AI is widely used for content generation, including articles, blog posts, social media content, and even scripts. By crafting precise and targeted prompts, users can guide the AI to produce high-quality, relevant text quickly. For instance, instead of asking the AI to "write an article," a more specific prompt such as "Write a 500-word blog post on the benefits of renewable energy, focusing on solar power" will yield a more focused and useful output.

Data Analysis

AI can assist in analyzing large datasets by generating summaries, highlighting key insights, or even making predictions based on trends.

With the right prompts, users can ask the AI to process complex data and provide actionable insights in plain language. For example, a prompt like "Summarize the sales trends for the last quarter and identify key areas for growth" can guide the AI to deliver an analytical summary of the data provided.

Customer Service and Support

Generative AI is increasingly used in customer service applications to generate responses to customer inquiries. By providing AI with well-crafted prompts, businesses can ensure that their AI-powered customer service tools offer quick, accurate, and personalized responses. For instance, a prompt such as "Generate a response to a customer asking for a refund on a late delivery" will result in an appropriate response that addresses the issue effectively.

Education and Training

AI can be used to create educational materials, provide tutoring, or even generate quizzes and tests. Teachers and trainers can craft prompts to generate study guides or interactive exercises. A prompt like "Create a 10-question multiple-choice quiz on the topic of World War II, covering key battles, leaders, and dates" will produce a tailored quiz to assess student knowledge.

Creative Writing and Storytelling

AI is also widely used in the creative fields, particularly in generating ideas for stories, plotlines, or character development. Prompts like "Write a science fiction short story about a time traveler who accidentally alters history" help writers overcome creative blocks and generate fresh ideas.

By tailoring the prompt to the desired outcome, users can unlock a wealth of creative, practical, and analytical capabilities of generative AI.

Multiple-Choice Questions: Practical Applications of Prompting

1. Which of the following best illustrates how prompting can assist in content creation?

A) Asking the AI to generate random text

B) Asking the AI to write a 500-word article on a specific topic with clear focus

C) Asking the AI to summarize a book without specifying any details

D) Asking the AI to analyze a list of keywords without context

2. How can generative AI be applied in data analysis?

A) By generating random data sets

B) By summarizing complex data and highlighting key insights

C) By making visualizations for data without prompts

D) By randomly categorizing data points

3. Which of the following prompts is most appropriate for customer service?

A) "How to resolve customer complaints"

B) "Generate a response to a customer asking for a refund on a late delivery"

C) "Create an advertisement for a new product"

D) "Write a guide for customer service representatives"

4. What is an example of how AI can be used in education and training?

A) Generating random questions for quizzes

B) Writing a lesson plan on a broad topic

C) Creating a customized quiz on a specific topic like World War II

D) Generating promotional materials for educational courses

5. How can prompting help in the field of creative writing?

A) By generating random character names

B) By offering suggestions for a plotline or story theme

C) By writing a book without any input

D) By providing factual information for writing

Answers

1. B 2. B 3. B 4. C 5. B

6. COMMON CHALLENGES IN PROMPTING

While prompting is an essential skill in utilizing generative AI, users often face several challenges that can affect the quality and relevance of AI-generated responses. These challenges can stem from unclear or overly broad prompts, a lack of understanding of the AI's capabilities, and issues related to bias or ethics.

Vague or Overly General Prompts

One of the most common challenges in prompting is the use of vague or overly broad prompts. Asking the AI to "Write an article" without any further direction often leads to generic and unfocused results. To achieve better results, prompts should be specific, outlining the topic, tone, length, and any other relevant parameters. For instance, instead of saying "Create a story," a more detailed prompt such as "Write a 1,000-word mystery story set in Accra, Ghana featuring a detective named Kofi" will provide clearer, more targeted results.

Difficulty in Achieving Desired Output

Another challenge is when the AI does not generate the expected or desired output. This can happen for a variety of reasons, including ambiguous instructions, the AI's interpretation of the prompt, or the limitations of the model. Sometimes, users may need to experiment with phrasing or provide additional context to clarify their request. For instance, a prompt like "Explain quantum mechanics" might be too broad, while "Explain quantum mechanics to a 10-year-old" offers more guidance.

Bias in AI Responses

AI systems are trained on vast datasets, some of which may contain biases, leading the AI to generate biased or harmful responses. This can be particularly problematic in sensitive topics, where a lack of diversity or balanced viewpoints might emerge. It's important for users to be aware of potential biases in the responses generated and take steps to mitigate these issues, such as carefully framing the prompt to avoid prompting harmful stereotypes.

Ethical Considerations

The ethical use of generative AI is another important challenge. Users must ensure that the AI-generated content is used responsibly and ethically.

For example, using AI to create fake news, manipulate opinions, or plagiarize content is not only unethical but can have significant real-world consequences.

It's important to always use generative AI in ways that align with ethical standards and societal norms.

Understanding AI's Limitations

Finally, one of the biggest challenges in prompting is understanding the limitations of the AI system. While generative AI is powerful, it is not infallible and may not always provide correct or reliable information. For example, asking an AI to solve a complex chemical engineering equation might result in errors, or asking it to generate a novel solution to a deeply technical problem might yield suboptimal results. Users must remain critical and validate the output, especially when dealing with high-stakes or technical applications.

Multiple-Choice Questions: Common Challenges in Prompting

1. Which of the following is a challenge that can occur when using vague prompts?

   A) The AI will provide specific results

   B) The AI may generate irrelevant or generic content

   C) The AI will always understand the intent

   D) The AI will refuse to generate any content

2. What is a potential reason why an AI might not generate the desired output?

   A) Ambiguous instructions or lack of context

   B) The AI has no understanding of the task

   C) The AI is designed to generate random content

   D) The AI generates perfect responses every time

3. How can bias manifest in AI-generated responses?

   A) The AI will always provide a balanced viewpoint

   B) The AI may generate biased or harmful content based on the training data

   C) The AI avoids controversial topics

D) The AI can only generate factual content

4. What is one example of an unethical use of generative AI?

A) Writing a customer service response

B) Using AI to create fake news or manipulate opinions

C) Generating educational materials for students

D) Creating art for personal use

5. Why is it important for users to understand the limitations of generative AI?

A) To ensure that AI always provides perfect answers

B) To validate and cross-check AI-generated content, especially in crucial scenarios

C) To use AI for creating unreliable information

D) To avoid using AI in any situation

Answers

1. B 2. A 3. B 4. B 5. B

7. ETHICAL USE OF GENERATIVE AI

Generative AI offers immense potential in transforming various fields, from content creation to customer service. However, as with any tool, its ethical use is crucial in ensuring that it benefits society while avoiding harmful consequences. In this section, we will explore key ethical considerations related to the use of generative AI and how users can ensure that their AI-generated content adheres to ethical standards.

Avoiding Harmful Content

One of the primary ethical concerns with generative AI is the potential for generating harmful, misleading, or offensive content. AI models can inadvertently produce content that is biased, discriminatory, or perpetuates harmful stereotypes if the data used to train the model contains such biases. To mitigate this risk, users must carefully craft prompts that avoid encouraging or reinforcing negative behaviors.

Additionally, the content generated should always be reviewed before sharing, especially when dealing with sensitive topics such as race, gender, religion, and politics.

Transparency and Accountability

It is essential for users to maintain transparency regarding the use of AI-generated content. If AI is used to create content such as articles, social media posts, or news stories, the audience should be informed that the content was generated with the assistance of AI. This transparency helps build trust and allows users to assess the reliability and context of the information presented. Moreover, users must take responsibility for how AI-generated content is used, ensuring that it does not deceive or mislead others, especially when it comes to crucial areas like healthcare, finance, or legal matters.

Intellectual Property and Plagiarism

Another important ethical consideration is the issue of intellectual property. Since generative AI can create content based on vast datasets, it can sometimes produce outputs that resemble existing works, raising questions about ownership and plagiarism. To avoid ethical dilemmas, it is crucial for users to verify the originality of AI-generated content.

Whenever possible, it is advisable to credit AI tools used in content creation, especially when incorporating their outputs into commercial products or public-facing materials. Additionally, users should avoid using AI to replicate or plagiarize the work of others.

Privacy and Data Security

Generative AI models are often trained on vast amounts of data, which may include personal information. While most AI tools are designed to respect privacy, users must be cautious not to prompt AI systems to generate content that could compromise privacy or violate data security protocols. For example, generating content that involves private individuals, confidential information, or proprietary data could lead to breaches of privacy laws and ethical guidelines. Users should ensure that they do not inadvertently expose sensitive or confidential information through AI-generated content.

Promoting Positive Outcomes

Generative AI should be used to promote positive social, cultural, and economic outcomes. AI-generated content can be a force for good, helping to educate, inform, entertain, and inspire.

Whether it's creating educational resources, assisting with social causes, or generating art that sparks creativity, users should aim to use AI in ways that contribute positively to society. Ethical use of AI involves using the tool for the greater good and avoiding applications that could harm individuals or communities.

Multiple-Choice Questions: Ethical Use of Generative AI

1. Which of the following is a key ethical consideration when using generative AI?

A) Using AI to generate content without reviewing it

B) Avoiding harmful, biased, or discriminatory content

C) Allowing AI to create content that may mislead or deceive

D) Using AI to automatically generate content for any purpose

2. What should users do to maintain transparency when using AI to create content?

A) Keep the use of AI hidden from the audience

B) Inform the audience that the content was generated with AI assistance

C) Use AI to generate content without any attribution

D) Disguise AI-generated content as human-made

3. How can users avoid ethical issues related to intellectual property when using generative AI?

A) Relying solely on AI-generated content without verification

B) Ensuring that AI-generated content does not plagiarize existing works

C) Sharing AI-generated content without crediting the AI tool

D) Using AI to duplicate existing content without permission

4. What should users do to ensure that generative AI does not violate privacy or data security?

A) Use AI to generate content involving private individuals or confidential information

B) Ensure that AI-generated content does not expose sensitive or proprietary data

C) Share AI-generated content without considering privacy issues

D) Ignore the potential privacy risks in AI-generated content

5. Which of the following best describes the ethical use of generative AI?

A) Using AI to deceive or manipulate people

B) Using AI to generate content that benefits society positively

C) Generating content without reviewing it for accuracy or ethical concerns

D) Encouraging harmful or unethical behaviors through AI content

Answers

1. B 2. B 3. B 4. B 5. B

8. PROMPT ENGINEERING: A LOOK AHEAD

Prompt engineering is the art and science of crafting effective prompts to guide AI models in producing the desired outcomes. As generative AI continues to evolve, prompt engineering will become an increasingly important skill for users across various industries. In this section, we will briefly explore the future of prompt engineering, how it will evolve, and the skills that will be essential for mastering this technique.

Advancements in AI Model Capabilities

As AI models improve, the ability to handle more complex and nuanced prompts will increase. Future AI systems will likely be better at understanding context, generating multi-step reasoning, and maintaining coherence over longer outputs. This advancement will require users to develop more sophisticated prompting strategies, such as breaking down complex tasks into smaller, manageable steps and providing clear contextual information in their prompts. The future of prompt engineering will involve leveraging these advanced capabilities to achieve more refined and targeted results.

Dynamic and Adaptive Prompts

In the future, prompts may become more dynamic and adaptive. This means that rather than relying on static instructions, users will be able to interact with AI in real-time, adjusting prompts based on the responses received. For example, a user might start by asking the AI for a general overview of a topic, and then refine the prompt to focus on specific subtopics based on the AI's initial response. This iterative approach will enable more personalized and adaptive outputs, allowing users to guide the AI in a more interactive and engaging manner.

Integration with Other Technologies

Prompt engineering will also evolve as generative AI becomes integrated with other technologies. For instance, AI tools could be integrated with natural language processing systems, machine learning algorithms, and even augmented reality (AR) and virtual reality (VR) environments. This convergence of technologies will create new opportunities for prompt engineering, where users can craft prompts that interact with multiple technologies at once, producing more immersive and complex experiences. For example, a prompt might instruct an AI to generate content that not only provides information but also triggers interactive visualizations in AR or VR.

Ethical and Responsible Prompt Engineering

As prompt engineering continues to evolve, so too must the ethical considerations concerning it. Users will need to be increasingly mindful of the implications of their prompts, ensuring that they do not inadvertently generate harmful, biased, or unethical content. This will require prompt engineers to consider the broader societal impact of the content generated and to adopt responsible practices when crafting prompts. The future of prompt engineering will likely involve greater emphasis on ethical responsibility, with tools and guidelines emerging to help users navigate these challenges.

Specialized Roles in Prompt Engineering

With the growing importance of prompt engineering, specialized roles and careers will emerge in the field. Companies and organizations will look to hire experts in prompt design who can create highly effective prompts for specific industries, such as healthcare, law, entertainment, and more. These roles will require not only technical knowledge of AI systems but also an understanding of the unique challenges and ethical considerations associated with different fields. Prompt engineers will need to collaborate with AI developers, data scientists, and subject matter experts to create tailored prompts that meet industry-specific needs.

Multiple-Choice Questions: Prompt Engineering: A Look Ahead

1. What is expected to happen as AI models continue to improve?

A) AI models will become less capable of handling complex prompts

B) AI models will become better at understanding context and generating coherent responses

C) AI models will stop working on multi-step tasks

D) AI models will only respond to very basic prompts

2. How might prompt engineering evolve in the future?

A) Prompts will remain static and not require updates

B) Prompts will become more dynamic and adaptive, allowing for real-time adjustments

C) Prompts will no longer need to be crafted at all

D) Prompts will become less interactive and more rigid

3. What is one potential application of prompt engineering as AI integrates with other technologies?

A) Using AI to generate simple text-based content only

B) Creating interactive visualizations in AR or VR through prompt instructions

C) Generating only static written content without integration with other technologies

D) Using AI exclusively for data analysis without any creative outputs

4. What will be a key ethical consideration in the future of prompt engineering?

A) Encouraging users to create prompts that generate biased content

B) Ignoring the impact of prompts on broader societal issues

C) Ensuring prompts are crafted responsibly to avoid harmful or unethical outcomes

D) Avoiding any ethical responsibility when using generative AI tools

5. What type of roles will likely emerge as prompt engineering becomes more important?

A) Roles focused on managing data storage only

B) Specialized roles focused on creating effective prompts for specific industries

C) Roles focused solely on coding AI models without any focus on prompts

D) Roles that ignore the unique challenges of different industries

Answers

1. B
2. B
3. B
4. C
5. B

9. MULTIPLE-CHOICE QUESTIONS AND ANSWERS

Here are 30 multiple-choice questions that cover all sections in the table of contents of this book. The questions are designed to assess both foundational knowledge and critical understanding of the content from all sections.

Introduction to Generative AI and Prompting

1. What is generative AI primarily used for?
   A) Generating hardware solutions
   B) Creating content based on data input
   C) Analyzing large datasets
   D) Predicting future trends

Answer: B) Creating content based on data input

2. What does a prompt do in the context of generative AI?
   A) It creates a dataset for training the model
   B) It guides the AI to generate a specific output
   C) It analyzes the generated content
   D) It filters the model's training data

Answer: B) It guides the AI to generate a specific output

Core Principles of Effective Prompting

3. Which of the following is crucial for an effective prompt?

A) The length of the prompt

B) Clear and concise instructions

C) Randomized inputs

D) Use of complex language

Answer: B) Clear and concise instructions

4. Why is context important in prompting generative AI?

A) To confuse the AI into providing creative answers

B) To ensure the AI can produce relevant and coherent outputs

C) To simplify the task for the AI

D) To make the AI generate random outputs

Answer: B) To ensure the AI can produce relevant and coherent outputs

Types of Prompts

5. Which type of prompt is best suited for a specific request or task?

A) Open-ended prompt

B) Goal-oriented prompt

C) Randomized prompt

D) All of the above

Answer: B) Goal-oriented prompt

6. An open-ended prompt is useful for generating what type of content?

A) Very structured responses

B) Creative, varied, and expansive outputs

C) Single-answer responses

D) Technical instructions

Answer: B) Creative, varied, and expansive outputs

Techniques to Improve Prompting

7. Which technique can help ensure a more accurate AI response?

A) Keeping the prompt vague and general

B) Providing additional context and details in the prompt

C) Asking for only short responses

D) Using technical jargon in the prompt

Answer: B) Providing additional context and details in the prompt

8. What is the benefit of using step-by-step prompting?

A) It speeds up the generation process

B) It helps the AI break down complex tasks into manageable parts

C) It ensures that the output is less creative

D) It reduces the need for input refinement

Answer: B) It helps the AI break down complex tasks into manageable parts

Practical Applications of Prompting

9. How can generative AI assist in content creation?

A) By directly replacing human writers

B) By generating ideas, drafts, or even final versions of content

C) By predicting trends based on personal preferences

D) By reducing the need for human creativity

Answer: B) By generating ideas, drafts, or even final versions of content

10. Which application is most suitable for AI-powered chatbots?

A) Content creation for blogs

B) Customer service and support

C) Data analytics

D) Financial forecasting

Answer: B) Customer service and support

Common Challenges in Prompting

11. What is a common challenge when prompting

generative AI?

A) Generating extremely detailed and precise outputs

B) Producing relevant and coherent responses

C) AI generating responses with too much context

D) Requiring fewer prompts to produce complex results

Answer: B) Producing relevant and coherent responses

12. How can biases in AI responses be minimized?

A) By using random inputs in prompts

B) By reviewing outputs before sharing them

C) By providing vague prompts

D) By avoiding the use of ethical considerations

Answer: B) By reviewing outputs before sharing them

Ethical Use of Generative AI

13. Which ethical consideration is important when using generative AI?

A) Creating as much content as possible without review

B) Avoiding harmful, biased, or discriminatory content

C) Keeping AI use hidden from the audience

D) Using AI exclusively for commercial purposes

Answer: B) Avoiding harmful, biased, or discriminatory content

14. Why is transparency important in generative AI?

A) It allows AI to work more efficiently

B) It helps build trust with the audience

C) It eliminates the need for context

D) It prevents AI from generating content

Answer: B) It helps build trust with the audience

Prompt Engineering: A Look Ahead

15. What is expected as AI models improve in the future?

A) They will become worse at handling complex tasks

B) They will be able to generate only short, simple outputs

C) They will be better at understanding context and generating coherent responses

D) They will eliminate the need for prompt engineering

Answer: C) They will be better at understanding context and generating coherent responses

16. What role might specialized prompt engineers play in the future?

A) They will only assist in data collection for training models

B) They will focus on creating effective prompts for specific industries

C) They will write AI algorithms from scratch

D) They will become obsolete as AI develops its own prompts

Answer: B) They will focus on creating effective prompts for specific industries

Bonus Questions for All Sections

17. Which of the following is essential for creating an effective prompt for generative AI?

A) It should be vague to allow for creativity

B) It should include specific instructions and context

C) It should avoid including too much detail

D) It should use as few words as possible

Answer: B) It should include specific instructions and context

18. What is one of the key features of a goal-oriented prompt?

A) It generates open-ended, creative responses

B) It guides the AI toward producing a specific output

C) It does not require any context to work effectively

D) It produces random results every time

Answer: B) It guides the AI toward producing a specific output

19. Which technique is most likely to improve AI responses?

A) Keeping the prompt ambiguous

B) Adding context and detailed instructions

C) Limiting the use of language variety

D) Using only short prompts

Answer: B) Adding context and detailed instructions

20. Which type of prompt would you use for a brainstorming session?

A) Goal-oriented prompt

B) Open-ended prompt

C) Step-by-step prompt

D) None of the above

Answer: B) Open-ended prompt

21. How does the iterative approach to prompting help improve AI-generated results?

A) By allowing for real-time adjustments based on feedback

B) By requiring users to input the same prompt repeatedly

C) By generating more creative responses

D) By limiting AI outputs to one sentence

Answer: A) By allowing for real-time adjustments based on feedback

22. Which of the following is an example of responsible AI use?

A) Using AI to spread misinformation

B) Generating content that promotes biased opinions

C) Ensuring AI-generated content is accurate and ethical

D) Using AI tools without review or oversight

Answer: C) Ensuring AI-generated content is accurate and ethical

23. How can generative AI help in content creation?

A) By eliminating the need for human input

B) By generating new content based on data provided by humans

C) By solely analyzing large datasets

D) By producing complex technical solutions

Answer: B) By generating new content based on data provided by humans

24. What is the primary goal of prompt engineering?

A) To train AI models directly

B) To create prompts that elicit specific, relevant responses

C) To evaluate AI models' performance

D) To manage data used for training

Answer: B) To create prompts that elicit specific, relevant responses

25. Which application can benefit from generative AI in customer service?

A) AI-powered chatbots

B) AI for financial analysis

C) AI for hardware design

D) AI for controlling manufacturing processes

Answer: A) AI-powered chatbots

26. What is the importance of transparency in generative AI outputs?

A) To ensure the AI works faster

B) To help users understand how outputs are generated

C) To avoid the need for human review

D) To prevent bias in AI responses

Answer: B) To help users understand how outputs are generated

27. What is an essential consideration when using generative AI ethically?

A) Generating content quickly, regardless of quality

B) Avoiding any form of oversight in AI outputs

C) Avoiding generating harmful or biased content

D) Encouraging the AI to generate content without context

Answer: C) Avoiding generating harmful or biased content

28. Which of the following will likely be a major focus in the future of prompt engineering?

A) Improving AI's ability to generate random responses

B) Increasing the complexity of prompts to confuse the AI

C) Ensuring prompts are tailored to specific industries and needs

D) Limiting the use of AI in content creation

Answer: C) Ensuring prompts are tailored to specific industries and needs

29. Why should AI-generated content be reviewed?

A) To ensure it fits specific industry requirements

B) To avoid errors or biases in the content

C) To make the content more creative

D) To make the content shorter

Answer: B) To avoid errors or biases in the content

30. What does the future of generative AI likely hold in

terms of prompts?

A) More complex prompts with less user involvement

B) A move towards simplified prompts with less detail

C) Increasingly sophisticated prompts tailored for specific tasks

D) Elimination of prompt engineering altogether

Answer: C) Increasingly sophisticated prompts tailored for specific

ABOUT THE AUTHOR

Dr. Kevin Abankwa's research focuses on business and big data analytics, with extensive professional experience in data strategy, governance, and advanced analytics. His career spans leadership roles in data-driven initiatives that optimize operations, improve decision-making, and foster innovation across industries.

Beyond his professional achievements, Dr. Abankwa is passionate about education and mentoring, bringing real-world expertise to the classroom to inspire the next generation of learners. As an adjunct faculty member at Central Piedmont Community College where he teaches a course on Artificial Intelligence, he is excited to share his knowledge and engage with students in and out of the classroom in meaningful and impactful ways.

www.ingramcontent.com/pod-product-compliance
Lightning Source LLC
LaVergne TN
LVHW022028200926
848481LV00007B/2593

* 9 7 9 8 9 8 7 9 1 8 9 0 6 *